Mental Legacy

Mental Legacy

Discover the Emotional and Mental Skills to Overcome Adversity in Life

Rudy S. Montijo, Jr.

Published by Game Changer Publishing
Cover Design: Skylar Cawley

Paperback ISBN: 978-1-962656-87-0
Hardcover ISBN: 978-1-962656-88-7
Digital: ISBN: 978-1-962656-89-4

www.GameChangerPublishing.com

DEDICATION

This book is dedicated to my family.

To my father: You've shown me how to turn a curse into a gift. You showed me recovery was obtainable and what was possible in my life. Your ability to connect with people and be compassionate, empathetic, and patient are characteristics I strive to obtain. You've given me your drive and your grit. You've given when you had nothing to give. You showed me the work ethic and discipline it takes to not only stay sober but to succeed. To take risks, bet on yourself, and support those who can't always support themselves. You've given me perspective. The sacrifices you've given so selflessly are felt by the countless lives you touch. If I can impact half the people you have, my goal will be reached. You taught me how to be a man. I love you.

To my mother: You are the first and last call of the day. No matter where in the world I was, you made sure I had a birthday cake with a candle on my birthday. But not just for me but for many of our family and friends. You've shown me the importance of celebrating people. Making them feel special because they are. You cared for and nurtured me, my brother and sister, and our kids. Customizing towels or travel bags. Anything that showed you put thought and care into it. All while working and returning to school to get your bachelor's degree. You taught me to work not until I'm tired but until the job is done. And it's never done. So there is always work to do. Mom, I'm not finished. I love you.

To my sister: You are strong. Much stronger than I have ever said and much stronger than you know. You've overcome adversity with poise and grace and were an inspiration to me as I fought my own battles. Your soul is warm, your heart is gold, and love is felt by all you touch. You've taught me to smile in bad times, laugh in the good, and never give up. You've shown up in my darkest hour and lit the path to a brighter day. You've given me strength I didn't have with the humbleness I need. You held my hand and looked after me as a child and supported and inspired me as a man. You are my sister, and I love you.

To my brother: You've given me more advice than I've ever given you. I've learned more about relationships, parenting, bravery, and honesty by watching your actions. You easily separate logic and emotion, a skill I teach, yet I'm still trying to master. You lead with love, not fear, which is why you succeed. You've led your big brother more than you know. I want to be like you when I grow up: intelligent, hard-working, amazing husband and an incredible father. You've set the bar so high I could never touch it. I will try. Your candor has kept me grounded, while your love has kept me lifted. You are my brother, and I love you.

To my daughter: You've taught me how to be gentle. You've softened my heart and forever changed how I interact with the world. At three years old, you are your own person. Witty, clever, intelligent, and beautiful. You're a princess, a unicorn, a mermaid, and whatever your heart and mind can think of, you can be. You've given me the gift of being a child again: to look at the world through kind eyes, a curious mind, and a warm heart. You are brave. You are strong. You are selfless. You are compassionate. You've taught me how to be all these things all over again. You will always be my little girl, and Daddy loves you with all his heart. Thank you.

To my son: You gave me the gift of being a father for the first time. With this gift came a love I never knew existed. Your deep laughter, radiant smile, and natural charisma draw attention wherever you are. You are a leader, and so you taught me to lead. You show your emotions, which taught me it was okay to show mine. You made me a protector and a fighter. You've given me patience and understanding. You've given me pride and humility, and when I drop to one knee to look you in the eye, you provide me with gratitude for everything I have and do not have in this world. You are my son, and you will guide me as much as I will guide you. I love you with all my heart. Thank you.

Read This First

Just to say thanks for buying and reading my book, I would like to offer you a few free bonus gifts, no strings attached! These gifts will help you get the most out of the steps in this book, and you can start using them immediately.

To Download Your Free Gifts, Scan the QR Code:

Mental Legacy

Discover the Emotional and Mental Skills
to Overcome Adversity in Life

Rudy S. Montijo, Jr.

www.GameChangerPublishing.com

Table of Contents

Introduction

August 12th, 2013.

I opened my eyes to find my car spinning in a dust cloud. Somehow, I managed to get to the side of the road. As the dust settled, I opened my door and stepped out. Looking around, I saw no one else. Walking around the car, I noticed my tires were blown out and the rims cracked. I couldn't drive away from this. Thankfully, no one was hurt. Soon, a police officer pulled up behind me. As the first officer stepped out, I waved him off, informing him that I had called a tow truck. The second officer approached me, immediately detecting the smell of alcohol. He handcuffed me, read me my rights, and placed me in the back of the squad car.

I yell out, "Hey, I hurt my neck in the accident. I need to go to the hospital."

Little did I know this last-ditch effort to get out of trouble would save my life. The ambulance arrived, and the paramedics loaded me onto the stretcher with my head in a brace. I asked them to call my parents. When my mom answered, I told her it had happened again. The paramedic took the phone and informed them we were headed to John C. Lincoln Deer Valley Hospital. I get rolled into the ER on a stretcher and put into a bay. Chaos is all around me. I hear nurses and doctors speaking quickly around me. A bright light is shining on my face, and then someone taps on my sternum… and everything goes black.

What just happened? Ten months earlier, I had started my dream job at one of the world's top medical device companies. I moved to Phoenix to start my new life. At 33, I thought I had finally grown up. Yet there I was, lying in a hospital bed with my arm handcuffed to it, a police officer in one corner of the room and my parents in another. They weren't upset; they were crying and scared.

What is it going to take for me to accept that I can't safely drink alcohol? I thought to myself.

A nurse approached the foot of my bed and asked if I could explain what happened. I told her what I could remember: I started at a restaurant in the Biltmore area, drinking a martini, when there was an accident, and then darkness.

She explained, "That darkness was when you stopped breathing and had to be intubated."

I had overdosed on alcohol. Alcohol had slowed my body's response systems to the point where I couldn't breathe on my own. She asked what I wanted to do next—be released or go to detox. This was my moment of reckoning; this was my opportunity to change. This was the moment I decided whether to choose life or to die a slow, painful, regretful death. I chose life.

I gave my parents the number to HR so they could call my company and try to save my job by letting them know I was going away for treatment. I was transported by ambulance to Valley Detox. My dad checked me in, and they confiscated anything I could harm myself with; they even took my shoelaces. He returned with a Walmart bag, handing me a pair of shorts, underwear, socks, and a T-shirt. The large metal door closed. There was a window in the door, reinforced with wire. We looked at each other through the glass, tears in our eyes. My dad, with now 42 years of sobriety, also struggled with alcoholism but was in recovery. His biggest fear had almost come true. He knew there was nothing he could do for me, nothing anyone could do. It was up to me and God.

It was within these white walls I conceded what everyone else already knew. I was an alcoholic. I accepted this for the first time in my life. This wasn't my first time attempting sobriety. However, it was the first time I truly accepted that I could not drink like ordinary people. I had no more ego when it came to alcohol. The facts spoke for themselves. It was time to be accountable. It was time to move forward. It was time to change. This was one of the best days of my life.

I would go to treatment and spend the next decade trying to be better, to learn, to grow, and achieve what I was capable of. It wasn't perfect. I want to say I never drank again after that, but that's not the truth. I've had my relapses. Will I have another? I don't know. I know I won't today. Tomorrow, probably not, but I will deal with that tomorrow.

I'm going to share my process with you. It is the culmination of over ten years of personal development. I've spent more than $200,000 on rehab, therapists, school, coaching, books, and anything and everything I could absorb to obtain the skills I needed—not just to survive, but to thrive in life. I've taken my experiences and what I've

RUDY S. MONTIJO, JR.

learned and created a process that anyone can quickly learn to overcome whatever adversity they face. This includes skills and a mindset that can be learned and taught to someone else, passed from one person to the next, leaving a legacy—a *Mental Legacy*. The *Mental Legacy* process transformed me from an alcoholic to an Ironman. The skills I've learned and the process I've created took me from being broken, in debt, and lost in life to becoming a loving father, son, brother, and friend. I've become a consistent top performer in my field, an entrepreneur, a competitive triathlete, financially stable, and a therapist. These skills have helped me navigate life, overcome adversity, and thrive with an inner peace and confidence in myself I've never known before. Now, I'm passing them on to you.

(NOTE: I've included a transcript of interviews I did for the audiobook version of this manuscript below and at the end of certain chapters as a special bonus for my readers.)

INTERVIEWER: Wow, that was quite the intro. I know that's a lot to unpack and process. It definitely pulled on some emotional chords with me, and I'm sure, with many others. So, we know what happened, but what were you feeling? What happened afterward? What was going on in your mind?

RUDY: Yeah, you know, there were just so many things going on, and I experienced a range of emotions. Lying in the hospital bed with my parents in tears, I felt so bad for them—for what I had put them through. This wasn't the first time. They had received calls like this many times before; it's a parent's worst nightmare. Then there's the disappointment in myself because I just kept screwing up. Time and time again, I blew these huge opportunities I had. It started with not taking college football seriously. I mean, how many kids dream of playing for a major Division I program? I partied that away, and now, ten years later, I blew another life-changing opportunity. I had a job with one of the top medical device companies in the world, and I blew that. Then, the fear, right? I was drinking. I got in an accident, and I'm getting charged, so jail is inevitable. I'd lose my license, my job—everything was about to be gone.

At this point, I'm 33 years old, so I'm not a young kid anymore—you only get so many chances in life.

Then, fast forward a few days later, I checked into rehab. There were about 12 of us guys there. The sad part is that, of those guys, 4 or 5 have overdosed and are no longer with us. I lost track of a couple, and 4 or 5 of us have made it to the other side and are doing well, at least they were when I wrote this book.

My first night in rehab, I went to my room, dropped to my knees, started crying, and just asked for help. I cried out and prayed. I said, "I've done it my way, and this is where it led me. You take it all. I am done, and I let go." Once I did that, the fear, the anxiety, the sadness, it all lifted. It was gone almost instantly because I was doing what was right for the first time in a very long time. I knew if I just did that, everything would work out. I knew it wasn't going to be quick; it wasn't going to be easy, but I was okay with that. For the first time, I stopped pretending I could go on living the way I had been. This was the first time I felt peace.

What is a Mental Legacy?

leg·a·cy /ˈlegəsē/ *Noun: The long-lasting impact of particular events, actions, etc., that took place in the past, or of a person's life. (Oxford)*

Jackie Chan is one of the world's most famous martial artists and action movie stars. At the time of writing this, his net worth is believed to be around $400 million. When asked if he would leave his fortune to his children, he said no. Chan explained, "If he (his son) is capable, he can make his own money. If he is not, then he will just be wasting my money."

Only about 21% of millionaires inherited their wealth; the rest earned it themselves. What makes them successful has very little to do with money; this book also does not focus on that aspect. Most people will never attain that level of wealth, which is okay. In fact, it's more than okay. While money can provide a certain level of security, it does not equate to happiness.

In my inner circle, I have family and close friends who have minimal savings and basic retirement plans, as well as friends in influential societal positions with net worths in the hundreds of millions. Their happiness is not dictated by the balance of their bank accounts.

I lost a close friend to cancer; she was only 26, just married, and starting a new life with her husband. Her family was wealthy, the owner of a prominent film studio in Hollywood with every medical resource money could buy. It didn't matter. If I asked her parents if they would trade it all for another day with her, I'm confident they would rather live in a modest home for one more hug from her.

When husbands and wives pass away unexpectedly, they leave their families not only with the challenge of financial self-support but also with profound emotional and mental impacts. The resulting hurt, pain, and trauma can create a ripple effect, leaving scars that endure and influence future generations.

It's a familiar tale: marriages plagued by misery often prioritize "being successful" over family connections. I experienced a loss of connection and missed precious moments with my children. We're conditioned to work hard to support our families, and while I agree that this is crucial, I believe there's another aspect of legacy that is even more significant than financial inheritance. Without it, everything can be lost; with it, anything is achievable. This is the legacy of mindset and mental well-being—a *Mental Legacy*.

The great actor and martial artist Bruce Lee famously said, "Instead of buying your kids all the things you never had, you should teach them all the things you were never taught. Material wears out, but knowledge stays."

A *Mental Legacy* is an emotional intelligence. It's emotional and mental maturity. It's grit. It is being disciplined physically. It is accountability, acceptance, and patience. It's love and empathy. It's the ability to regulate emotions. It's the ability to overcome adversity, thrive in chaos, and discern facts from feelings. The power of self-awareness, not being a victim, and taking action to achieve a desired outcome. If applied, the stories and tools you're about to read and receive can help you overcome any adversity you might face—relationships, breakups, kids, addiction. You can expect to strengthen your marriage, be a more present parent and partner, succeed at work, eliminate debt, and gain wealth if you choose.

The goal is simple. Learn these simple skills to pass down to your children. That is creating a *Mental Legacy*.

The Process

Over the past decade on my journey, I've spent six figures and have been exposed to multiple modalities of treatment, therapy, coaching programs, and experiences. While on their own, each one serves a specific purpose, I found the nuances can become over-complicated and hard to digest. I created an acronym for each part of the *Mental Legacy* process to simplify this into a method anyone can use, remember, and (most importantly) apply.

E.N.L.I.T.E.N.

"E" is for **Ego** and accountability. To change or overcome any situation, we must first accept the reality of the problem. The acceptance piece is the only thing we can control, which is ourselves. Pointing the finger or passing blame is another way of deflecting and creating a victim mentality. Only when we understand what triggers the ego (defensiveness) and what lowers it can we truly see a situation for what it is rather than what we think it should be.

"N" stands for **Needs**, as in what *needs* to happen to reach a desired outcome. This is viewed from a macro (large scale) and micro (day-today) viewpoint. It becomes a constant reminder of why we are doing what we are doing when the activity becomes too routine or boring; understanding the "why" is crucial in achieving life's short-term and long-term goals and gives meaning to everything from our morning habits to our interactions with our spouse and children.

"L" stands for **Leadership**. These principles become your compass, the leadership type that leads your life first. After you master them, you'll lead others. Developing the traits you want to possess and exude will make it easier to make decisions. No more gray areas; how you live your life becomes black and white. You define your character by your actions and consistency.

"I" is for **Integration**. You understand how to use—integrate—these tools in different aspects of your life. No matter where you are, personally or professionally, you can dissect the situation and respond in a way that aligns with your goals and character.

"T" is for **Training** your **Thoughts**. Here, I break down the science behind creating new neural pathways in your brain leading to transformation and long-term change. You know it's working when the conscious thought becomes a subconscious reaction.

"E" is for **Emotions**. We dive deeper into why you feel the way you do. I put on my therapist hat to give a general background of how past trauma is playing a role in your present life. I will cover topics like attachments, abandonment, and fear vs. love and give resources to dive deeper on your own or with a therapist.

And finally, "N" stands for **Nurture**. The work never stops, and nurturing your heart and mind is critical. With your newfound appreciation for these skills, you can share your experience and help others. I've found this helps create empathy and compassion for those struggling and who might need a little help. Everyone has a time in their life where nurturing is beneficial.

This book is designed to be applied to your life immediately. I've included "notes" or journal pages throughout this book to help you get started. To effectively use this in your life, I've broken down each principle into three areas of life—personal, professional, and physical:

Personal is you, your relationship, emotions, mindset, addictions, or recovery. Your spiritual health, or if you're religious, it would fall under this as well.

Professional is your current job, where you want to be, the business you want to start, etc.

Physical refers to your physical health; I'm not talking about aesthetics—the outward appearance or the beauty of the body—but rather what is essential to your ability to thrive: your weight, sleep, diet, exercise, etc.

You should have goals in all three areas. It will most likely be multiple personal goals, a professional goal, and a physical goal. It should be something measurable to track your progress or identify areas that need attention. Examples include taking a trip with your wife by March 1st, paying off your credit card by October 10th, signing up for a race such as the P.F. Chang's Rock and Roll half or full marathon, or starting with a 5k or 10k.

You need a target for your brain to subconsciously and consciously focus on. You need to be intentional in your time. You cannot float through life like a ship with no sail. You'll end up somewhere you don't want to be and blame it on the wind or the waves. The truth is that you didn't have a rudder, a sail, a compass, or a destination. You ended up where you did because you didn't have a plan. You do now. Hopefully, so will your loved ones. The skills taught and passed down will be your legacy.

CHAPTER 1

Ego and Accountability

e·go /ˈēgō/ *Noun: A person's sense of self-esteem*
or self-importance. (Oxford)

ac·count·a·bil·i·ty /əˌkoun(t)əˈbilədē/ *Noun: The fact or*
condition of being accountable responsibility. (Oxford)

What is the Ego?

The ego is you. It's how you view yourself in relation to the external world. It is "self" and "I." It is commonly thought of as pride, which in turn reflects how we view ourselves.

The ego can be compared to an ever-shifting river current, subtly influencing everything in its path, yet often unnoticed. Picture the ego as this river current: sometimes it flows gently, almost imperceptibly, guiding things along its course. At other times, it can be turbulent, forcefully changing the direction of everything it touches. Just as it's challenging to identify the exact path and influence of a current beneath the water's surface, it's equally difficult to recognize our own ego or focus on someone else's. Nevertheless, like the relentless flow of a river, the ego in each of us is always active and influential, whether we acknowledge it or not.

The Ego Can Help and Hurt Us

When people refer to the ego, it is most commonly in a negative context. I'm sure you've said or heard someone say, "That person has a huge ego." It probably was not meant to be a compliment. But the ego is designed to keep you safe. Subconscious triggers can be activated, creating a reaction tied to childhood trauma or an event. This happens without us being aware or even having to think about it. These same "triggers" can also activate a not-so-helpful mechanism—being defensive, which I like to call the "wall of denial." Once the wall of denial goes up, it is extremely difficult for any information to enter or exit.

Have you ever talked with someone and they say something you disagree with? Right then, all you can think about is what you plan on saying to refute their argument when they stop talking. You can't wait to speak. If this is your thought process, you're not capable of listening with an open mind. Your wall of denial went up; new information wasn't received. Therefore, whatever you say won't be completely logical either. When your wall is up, you can't move; it blocks you from progressing and growing.

The goal is to become self-aware when the ego is engaged, or the wall of denial is activated, bringing it down so you can look at the world and yourself as you truly are. So, you can hear the conversation as it was said. You listen to facts, ask questions, learn, and think. You are teaching yourself to react with logic rather than emotion. Feelings aren't facts; they are just feelings. Acknowledging your imperfections and what you do not know is much more important than constantly reinforcing what you do.

What Does True Accountability Mean?

I've had many clients over the years, and one of the first exercises I have them do is to carry around a notebook for a week. Every time they complain or blame anything, no matter what, they write it down. This can be as trivial as complaining that the line in Starbucks took too long or that you're unhappy because your partner did something to you. If they do this and are honest about it, typically, they have a few pages full of complaints quickly. This can be eye-opening and shed some light on what's been going right and wrong in your life. Try not to rationalize or justify any of your complaints; get in the habit of owning your part and your part only.

Most people do not fully grasp the concept of accountability. One hundred percent accountability means being responsible for everything about yourself, the only thing in life you can control. This means whether your natural reaction is to complain about a long line, accept it and wait patiently, or perhaps use the extra time to educate yourself while you wait by listening to a podcast. It means recognizing that being with your partner is a choice you make voluntarily and that you have the freedom to leave at any moment rather than placing blame on them. Since you have chosen to be with this person, shouldn't you try to understand them and see them as they wish to be seen? It involves regulating your emotions, reactions, and thoughts so that your response is truly yours, not merely a reaction to something external or internal. This is a crucial piece of information: you need to discern whether you are responding in a certain way because of the current situation or due to something that happened in the past.

A quick example is you were cheated on in your last relationship. Your current partner always puts their phone screen on the table face down when you eat. A few things could happen here.

1. You begin to feel like they are hiding something, immediately question their intentions and trust, and spiral down a rabbit hole of "what ifs."

2. You recognize you're reacting to something that happened in the past. This person has not broken trust with you, so they don't deserve to feel the mistrust and judgment meant for someone else. If you can't let it go, communicate. "Hey, I noticed you sometimes put your phone screen down on the table when we're together. Mind if I ask why?" A normal response might be, "I get several messages and emails from work or friends during the day. I want to make sure I'm present and focused with you, so I put it down so I don't get distracted. If I'm expecting a message or email, I might leave it up so I don't miss time-sensitive information."

Hopefully, after that type of response, you will be reassured; over time, it will be less of an issue.

I understand that things happen in life that are not our fault, and many people are victims of circumstances beyond their control. I'm not minimizing anyone's personal situation or traumatic events. However, even in the most severe conditions, there are aspects we can control. Most importantly, what actions do we take afterward?

The Two Parts of Trauma

In their book, *The Myth of Normal,* Gabor and Daniel Maté describe two parts of trauma: the event that happens and the trauma that follows. The event can never be changed. It happened; that's it. Trauma is the harm or injury caused by the event. There is a third part to this, which is the effects or collateral trauma.

Imagine if you get into a car accident, break your leg, and strain some muscles. The car accident can never be changed; it happened and cannot be undone. We may or may not have controlled that. But if your leg is broken and your muscles are strained, you can see a doctor and have your leg set and cast. You can see a physical therapist to work through your muscle strain. If you treat your leg and do proper exercises to help your muscles, you will get better. You may have some scar tissue from the accident, so you will never forget it and will always know it happened.

However, this doesn't have to prevent you from walking again. Even if you cannot regain 100% of your previous ability, you can get close in most cases. Amputees still run marathons. You cannot change the car accident, but you can choose how to treat or not treat your leg if you want it to heal. There is a 3rd part of trauma, collateral trauma. You can develop these characteristics by not processing or healing from the event. This shows up in life as unhealthy attachments, lack of boundaries, narcissism, resentment, anger, and a fear-based perspective.

The same is true of emotional trauma. Whatever happened cannot be undone. The harm, the injury, and the aftermath can be acknowledged, processed, and worked through most times. That part is your choice. No money or insurance? Many states have free resources; many therapists have free YouTube channels where anyone can learn more about any topic and how to heal. I didn't say it would be easy, but it is possible if YOU choose. That's accountability. Talk to your ego. The ego isn't harmful or good. It just is. The critical part is building a healthy relationship with our ego. Identify when something is trying to help or hurt you and respond accordingly. The way you do this is to understand the signs when your ego is activated and what it means. Is your heart racing? Are you sweating? Do you feel angry, sad, or withdrawn and unsure why? Discovering what triggered these reactions is the next step—healing the injured inner part of yourself. We will cover this in-depth in *Chapter 6: Emotions*. This is not an overnight process; it will take time, but having awareness is the first step. The rest is practice.

Reclaim Your Power

Have you ever noticed how two different people react during an argument or debate? One person may become very emotional and upset, losing their cool and seeming as if they've lost control. The other person remains calm and calculated, choosing the right words and knowing exactly when to say them, appearing very much in control. Which one would you rather be?

In life, nine times out of ten, the first person loses. They could be a professional athlete getting a foul called for yelling at the ref. It could be a person getting mouthy with a police officer at a routine traffic stop or a job interview with tough questions. Suppose a person cannot, in real-time, identify the trigger, lower their ego, control their emotions, and respond, not react, which would be appropriate in the context. In that case, they cannot control themselves and the situation.

Suppose a person regulates their emotions, avoids that foul, communicates effectively, and answers the tricky question assertively and accurately. In that case, they will immediately control 50% of the situation; with some skill, even more. That is proper accountability. That is power. True power is understanding how much control you have over your life and having the skills to get where you want to go.

At Home Exercise: Here is a simple exercise to do at home. I've left some space for you to make some notes. I want you to pay close attention every time something causes you to get defensive and every time you complain or blame someone or something. Watching FOX or CNN news and something upsets you. Write it down. Talking to a friend or co-worker about something you disagree with, and you instantly want to defend your point of view? Write it down. In line at the grocery store, a person in front pulls out their checkbook. You think, *Oh my gosh, this person is so slow and ancient.* Write it down. Keep this going for a week. You'll be surprised what you find.

NOTES:

_____

_____

_____

_____

_____

_____

_____

_____

_____

_____

_____

_____

_____

_____

_____

_____

_____

_____

_____

_____

_____

_____

_____

_____

_____

_____

_____

_____

_____

_____

One of life's most important aspects is our relationships with others, but more importantly, with ourselves. I relapsed on alcohol in the summer of 2021. This dramatically shifted the trajectory of my life in a good way, though not without first navigating through some challenging times. I'll be general while still trying to use the **E.N.L.I.T.E.N.** process. I will be authentic and vulnerable with readers—being accountable and accepting—just as I ask of you.

E (EGO): I drank and lied about it. I failed to use the tools I had to avoid drinking. I chose an easier, temporary solution instead of doing what was difficult but necessary. I accept this.

N (NEEDS): Macro: I need to be sober. I need to get healthy in all areas of my life to be the best father for my children. Micro: Redo the 12 steps, attend AA, and work through the shame and guilt from the separation with my therapist. Process it healthily.

L (LEADERSHIP): I need to be patient, have gratitude, and prioritize critical parts of life.

I (INTEGRATION): As situations arise, I make sure I'm in communication with my therapist. I find meetings to go to while traveling and meet my sponsor regularly. I use the tools given at the appropriate time.

T (TRAIN YOUR THOUGHTS): Retrain my mind to meditate, pray, or go to a meeting or workout when triggered. This was a very volatile time, and I was triggered a lot. I began training for triathlons as an outlet in addition to other modalities of therapy.

E (EMOTIONS): Work with my therapist to identify why I was feeling and why I was feeling a certain way. I need to be accountable for my part and then repeat the process. I did EMDR and medically supervised ketamine therapy to help release and process emotions.

N (NURTURE): At this point, I just continued to repeat these steps to get back some mental and emotional stability.

Physical

My physical goal was to complete my first Ironman. An Ironman consists of three parts: a 2.4-mile swim, a 112-mile bike ride, and then a 26.2-mile run—a full marathon.

E: This was less about ego and more about being accountable for my training. I hired a coach because I knew I did not know what to do or expect.

N: I needed to train. I needed to make time to swim, bike, and run consistently. The macro goal is Ironman. Daily goals are each workout.

L: I needed to prioritize my training. I did this by setting a schedule. If something came up at the same time, I said no. "I can't. I have to train." No questions. I also took my running shoes with me on work trips and ran before or after work because I could not access a bike or swimming pool for laps. I needed to be consistent. I also explained to family and friends my goal and why I was trying to accomplish it. I told them I could not attend certain things because of my training regimen. They understood and supported me, rather than feeling like I avoided them or that something was wrong with the relationship.

I: I planned training around my work schedule and time with my kids. If I were staying in Tucson with my parents, I would ask if I could run early in the morning, and they would watch the kids for 20-30 minutes while I ran. Besides this, I rarely worked out when I had my kids unless it was on my Peloton while they slept.

T: I didn't always want to or even like working out. But I trained my mind to associate the feeling after you're done with starting. I would chase the dopamine you get from accomplishment. After a while, despite how tired I was and how much I didn't want to, I chose to do it. This is how I built my discipline over time, and it became second nature and just a part of my life.

E: Emotionally, there were a lot of ups and downs. The times I wanted to quit or said I was too stressed to train were all rooted in fear of not living up to my expectations and being embarrassed. I publicly said I was doing an Ironman. I talked about it all the time. So, at times, I kept looking for an "out." I learned to turn my fear into love and excitement. Countless times, I imagined how I would feel crossing that line and forever being called an Ironman.

N: I learned to repeat this cycle daily—talks with friends who encouraged me, my coach, and other triathletes. I gained confidence and encouraged others to train and sign up for races. If I were dating someone, we'd work out together. If my friend ran a 10k, I'd show up and support them.

(BONUS: Audiobook transcript)

INTERVIEWER: So, ego and accountability are the first part. Where did you come up with that? How has it, and does it play a role in your own life?

RUDY: Man, this is just the foundation for everything. It's an ongoing process to check yourself and really look within. The Ego part is really understanding yourself and accepting your flaws as a person, knowing your strengths and weaknesses, and being able to be honest about those going into every situation in life.

The accountability part is all about taking back control of your life. I got tired of blaming, making excuses of why this didn't happen or what happened to me. I realized I was the only person who could create the life I wanted, no one else. After rehab, I could have moved back to Tucson and leaned on family for help, but I thought, no way, man. You have to figure this out. So, I stayed in the Phoenix area and built my life here. Some might view that decision as scary, but if you really think about it, it's an amazing feeling to know you can control your future. You write your own story, and it ends any way you want. Accountability gives you your power and control back. When you have that, anything is possible.

CHAPTER 2

Needs/Desired Outcome

need /nēd/ *Noun: A requirement, necessary duty, or obligation; Necessity arising from the circumstances of a situation or case. (Oxford)*

You've started to become more self-aware, understanding your triggers and what puts your wall up. That's great! But what's next? What NEEDS to happen? Well, that depends on your desired outcome. Unlike a goal, the desired outcome is what you hope to achieve in a situation, not necessarily a pre-planned goal. This system works for both, but remember, the main objective is to apply this in real-time and daily. Let me explain.

A goal is what you write down and what you want to accomplish or obtain, and the outcome is what needs to happen on a daily basis to achieve the goal. The desired outcome occurs in the blink of an eye and is specific to a situation as it unfolds. Let's say your goal is to have a happy, healthy relationship, and when you inevitably argue, you aim to say nothing hurtful that could damage the relationship. Now that the argument has started, you must quickly figure out your desired outcome for this particular situation. If your desired outcome is to not worsen the situation, then you NEED to know what to do to achieve this. You might need just to be quiet and listen. You might need to say, "I'm sorry," or you might need to lean in for a hug—an underrated move to defuse situations. By not making the situation worse, you're letting your partner be seen and creating a safe place for vulnerability. This will help you accomplish your goal of building a happy and healthy relationship. Every time you reach your desired outcome in a specific situation, you're staying on track to accomplish your larger goal.

Macro and Micro

Macro refers to the big picture, a bird's-eye view, the overall goal. Macro means large. Micro involves the steps taken each day, the daily habits, the small details. Micro means small. Why is this important? As humans, we quickly forget; we lose motivation quickly. Understanding your MACRO goal will help give meaning to the MICRO steps needed to be accomplished, day in and day out, to meet your MACRO goal.

Let's break this down a little further. Let's say your MACRO goal is a happy, connected partnership. You can do many things to accomplish this, but you've decided to mail a handwritten card to your partner twice a month. You've put *"send card"* in your calendar. The alert pops up on your phone. At first, you ignore it, but then you see in the notes, *"Sending this card will let her know you care, even though life gets busy."* Sending the card is the MICRO action that helps to accomplish the MACRO goal.

Let's use another example. Let's say your child wants to make the varsity sports team or win the science fair. That is their goal. Breaking it down into smaller, obtainable goals will help. Practice for an hour after school. Test different experiments to see what works. On their own, it could become tiresome. Then, you remind them that each day they practice, or every experiment tested, leads to the larger goal. Give each day meaning. Give them one block. By itself, it is just a block. But fifty blocks built on top of one another can be a castle. This is the essence of micro and macro.

Do you want to move the needle even faster? Find out what the keystone habit is for each goal. What is a keystone habit?

Keystone Habit

A keystone habit is a powerful behavior that has the potential to trigger a chain reaction of positive changes in various aspects of your life. Coined by Charles Duhigg in his book *The Power of Habit*, a keystone habit is like a cornerstone that, when adopted and consistently practiced, can lead to the development of other positive habits and the transformation of your overall lifestyle.

The concept of a keystone habit is rooted in the idea that habits are interconnected. Focusing on changing one fundamental behavior can create a domino effect, influencing other aspects of your life. The keystone habit acts as a catalyst for broader, positive change.

One classic example of a keystone habit is regular exercise. When you commit to exercising consistently, it not only improves your physical health but also has a ripple effect on your mental and emotional well-being. Exercise often leads to better sleep, increased energy, and enhanced mood. This can positively impact your productivity, self-esteem, and overall outlook on life.

The key to the effectiveness of a keystone habit lies in its ability to trigger other positive behaviors. For example, exercising can act as a cue for other habits, such as making healthier dietary choices, managing stress more effectively, and maintaining a more organized schedule. This interconnected web of positive habits reinforces each other, creating a positive feedback loop that sustains the momentum for change.

Breaking old patterns with a keystone habit involves identifying behavior that has the potential to influence multiple aspects of your life. This requires self-reflection and an understanding of the habits you want to change. Once you've identified a suitable keystone habit, the next step is to start small. Setting achievable and realistic goals increases the likelihood of success and helps build confidence.

Consistency is critical when establishing a keystone habit. It's not about making drastic changes overnight but about sustainably incorporating the chosen behavior into your daily routine. Whether it's exercising for 20 minutes each day, meditating in the morning, or dedicating time to learning a new skill, the regularity of the habit fosters lasting change.

As the keystone habit becomes ingrained in your routine, you'll likely start noticing positive changes in other areas of your life. New, healthier habits gradually replace old patterns. The process is gradual, and setbacks may occur, but the focus remains on the overall trajectory of positive change.

A keystone habit serves as a linchpin for personal transformation. By strategically targeting and altering one core behavior, you set in motion a series of positive changes that extend beyond the initial habit. Breaking old patterns becomes a natural outcome of consistently practicing the keystone habit, creating a positive domino effect that can lead to a more fulfilling and balanced life.

Write down your goals. Start with one professional, personal, and physical goal, along with daily action steps to achieve these. Give yourself a deadline. Finding your keystone habit creates a waterfall effect of productivity.

(BONUS: Audiobook transcript)

INTERVIEWER: So, this seems relatively straightforward, but I think a lot of people might want to hear how you've used this to really grow and accomplish what you have, so they can do something they've only thought about, or maybe feel like their goal is unattainable.

RUDY: You're right, and I have to remind myself of this often because it didn't happen overnight, but it did happen. It's really simple if you just start from the end. There is a blueprint for life and success; most people just don't follow it or don't understand it. I didn't get it until I got sober. People look at a doctor and think, *Oh my God, how did you do that?* Well, it's easy when you break it down. It's time and effort. You have four years of undergraduate study, four years of medical school, residency, fellowship, or clinics, and you're a doctor. That's it.

Two of my friends from rehab literally started from nothing, and now they are doctors, and both doing very well. So, if you just start with what you need first. Well, I need a degree. Okay, go online and register for a class or two. Do that for a month, then a year, then apply to medical school, and do it all over again; eventually, you will be a doctor.

It's the same thing with Ironman. This, to me, seemed like just an insurmountable goal. I started to make excuses and not be accountable. I didn't know how I was going to do it or even if I would be able to finish. The first thing I did was commit. Then, for the full Ironman, I hired a coach, but you can go online and get free training programs. So, I broke it down day by day. This day, I swam; this day, I ran. I have kids part-time, and I travel a lot for work, so I only did about 60% of the workouts. On average, I'd say I worked out 3 or 4 days a week. But I was consistently working out 3 or 4 days a week, week after week, month after month, for one full year. Then race day came, and I was able to finish in just under 14 hours. You can apply this same strategy and mentality to any goal.

Now, here's the best part. When you start to accomplish something you haven't done before, your perception of what you're capable of changes. You think, *Okay, what else can I do? What else can I achieve?* You've just unlocked a tiny piece of potential and possibility. You build on that and don't look back, and before you know it, you'll have a confidence and self-esteem that you've never felt before.

This is part of what I teach in my video course because when you start being accountable and accomplishing your goals, all of a sudden, the anxiety goes away, the depression fades, and you start choosing different people to associate with, different people to date. You don't become a different person; you become the person you were meant to be. Everyone has that in them—everyone. Everyone's potential is different. I'm not naïve to the fact that some people are born with God-given abilities and under better or worse circumstances. We don't choose what we look like, how tall we are, where we are born, or to whom we are born. But at some point, we do have a choice. So, accept the reality and facts of your life. Stop blaming anyone and everyone. Then, start making decisions that will get you where you want to be. That's it.

At Home Exercise: Write down three goals: one personal, one professional, and one physical. Now, just break those down with the simplest step to complete each one for just one day. Saving money? Pack a lunch twice a week. Want to lose weight? Skip breakfast and take a 20-minute walk a day (consider listening to an audiobook).

NOTES:

_____

_____

_____

_____

_____

_____

_____

_____

_____

_____

_____

_____

CHAPTER 3

Leadership

lead·er·ship /ˈlēdərˌSHip/ *Noun: the action of leading
a group of people or an organization. (Oxford)*

When you think of a leader, who comes to mind? Perhaps someone like Nelson Mandela, Winston Churchill, Rosa Parks, or Princess Diana? If you're not thinking of yourself, we have a problem. How can you expect to lead your children, household, employees, or even yourself if you don't view yourself as a leader? You can't. However, you can begin to act and lead yourself in the direction you want more easily than you think. It starts with new character traits.

I first got this idea after reading *Ride of a Lifetime* by Bob Iger, CEO of Walt Disney, and *Principles* by Ray Dalio. We have to define the person we want to be; then, we come up with ten traits that guide our every decision. There is no gray area; this is black and white. We do not waver on this because if we do, we jeopardize our integrity. If we do that, our foundation weakens, leaving room for more compromises, and soon, we are back to living in confusion and digression. The following are the ten traits that I've created for myself. Feel free to take all ten, add, omit, or create a new list.

1. Self-Awareness

Self-awareness is the most essential and challenging trait to develop. We often see things as we want them to be, not as they are. Our perspective on life has been shaped by years of experience, how we were raised, and the traumas we've experienced, especially if they have not been processed.

The part of the country we come from, or even the country itself, also plays a role. A person raised in New York City or San Francisco most likely has very different views than those who grew up in Amarillo, Texas, or Little Rock, Arkansas. Children raised in poverty view life differently from those raised in wealth, and so on. Whatever a person's perspective is, it doesn't make it right or wrong; it just is. If you understand this, you can learn to listen objectively to others and make more unbiased decisions. Because much of this happens subconsciously, it's good to have third-party help, such as a therapist or people with no vested interest in you or your decisions.

A guru once said, "Your nose is right above your mouth, yet we cannot smell our breath… but others can." Understanding that you cannot see your blind spots and creating a plan to bring them to light is the first step to self-awareness.

2. Grit with Optimism

Life is hard and full of challenges. This will never change. We must decide how we will face these challenges, these lows. Will we complain and begrudgingly go through life, or will we understand that the pain is temporary? "This, too, shall pass." We should smile and maintain a positive attitude. Look, I'm not saying to ignore your feelings or reality, but we need not make it worse with a poor attitude when life gets tough. We can view everything as a learning opportunity, a chance to grow. We should process the emotions, then smile and move forward, knowing we will be okay! Or would you rather choose the alternative? The choice is yours.

Imagine the President saying, "Oh my gosh, I don't know what we're going to do. This country wants to cut off our oil."

Or a professional athlete saying, "I can't make the game because I'm too tired and need to stay home."

Or your child saying, "I won't move out and get a job because it's too hard to pay bills."

Start by being there for yourself first. When you reframe the situation, you see how and what you admire in others and what you don't. Be the person people turn to for support and hope through challenging times.

3. Takes Action - Be Decisive

Know yourself, and this task will be easy. Question yourself, and it won't be. The reason for having these traits and values listed is to eliminate the need for overthinking. I have my kids part-time. I plan my entire life around them. If a concert or a sporting event is coming to town and it's on a weekend when I have them, it's a no. That's it. My kids are my priority, so there's no need to think about it. If there's a bachelor party in Vegas where there will be an excess of everything, it's a no. "Sorry, man, but I'm going to pass; it doesn't sound like the best environment for my sobriety, but thank you, and I'll see you at the

41

wedding." I'm training for an Ironman. My workouts are planned. I don't deviate because I want to be ready on race day.

"Rudy, do you want to meet us for brunch at 10 a.m.?"

"Sorry, man, I have a ride that morning. Happy to make dinner, though." Done. No thought needed.

Another way to be decisive is by understanding and knowing your craft. Whatever your job or career is, become an expert so that you can confidently answer questions. If you don't know, you should know where to find the answer. Imagine asking your doctor about bloodwork you just had done, and they didn't know the answer. How much confidence would you have in them? The same applies to you. People admire and look to someone who takes action with decisiveness.

Here is a famous story to illustrate the importance of being decisive.

Norman Schwarzkopf, Commander-in-Chief during the Gulf War, used to tell a story about an early mentor of his, a general in the Army.

There was a decision regarding the politics of the war that had to be made. The importance of this decision lay in ten years of history, going back and forth with the Pentagon to decide whether they should go. It was a huge decision that would affect how the Army was structured. The highest-ranking officials brought enormous stacks of documents and complicated technical explanations.

The General just looked at them and said, "The answer is obvious, gentlemen." And he gave them the answer.

After they left, Schwarzkopf freaked out. He knew there was no way the general could have read everything he had. This was such a complex situation with so many parts to consider. Schwarzkopf, a much lower-ranked officer, summoned the courage to ask his mentor how he could have taken such decisive action. "There is so much information here; there's so much to consider, no one will know for sure. How the hell could you just make a decision like that?"

The General replied, "This has been a decision that no one's been willing to make for ten years. The best minds have been on it, and they can't decide, so you know what? We need to pick one and do it. Decisions are power, and I'm here to make them. That's why I'm in this position. That's why I'm a leader."

Schwarzkopf replied, "What if you're wrong?"

"If I'm wrong, we'll find out quicker," said the General, "and if I'm right, the job will be done."

Schwarzkopf never forgot that experience.

4. Consistency (Discipline)

You are going to mess up at first. It's okay; this is a lifelong process. You might have heard the saying, "People don't change." This is usually true, but only because most people never do the work required to change. I don't believe that people cannot change. People can and do change all the time. Ask anyone who knew me in my 20s and 30s and knows me now. I guarantee they will say I have changed. A lot! The only way to truly change and transform is to practice these things every hour, day, week, month, and year in every situation possible. Practicing these principles day in and day out will retrain your brain. (More on this later.)

Suppose you follow these steps and truly practice them. Over time, you will not be the same person. I know because I'm not the same person I was ten years ago or even two years ago. I would not want to be. That would mean I stopped growing, emotionally maturing, and still made the same mistakes without progressing. That's it. There may be times when we stumble and take a step back. This is normal. Don't be too hard on yourself, and don't stay there, either. Get back on track and try again.

Being consistent is much more than being disciplined to accomplish your goals. It defines your character; you are the sum of your actions. If you're in a relationship, don't just get flowers or open the door initially; do it throughout the entire relationship to establish a strong connection with your kids. Take the time each week or set a schedule to spend alone with them individually. But don't just do it for a month or two; do it every year. How you show up for people will build trust and strong relationships; if someone in your life is inconsistent with their behavior, ask yourself how large a role they should play, if any. Being predictable can be a good thing.

5. Empathy

Empathy is one of the most potent traits a person can have. It allows you to put yourself in someone else's shoes for a minute and try to see things from their perspective. It takes tremendous self-awareness and patience. Being empathetic means not judging others because we don't know their story. It means being patient with others because not everyone is like us. It means trying to connect on a basic human level. As humans, we all need food, shelter, stability, security, and love. Imagine what it must feel like to lack any of these things.

What would it be like not having enough money to feed your family? What would it feel like to be bouncing around as a kid from one home to the next? What would it feel like not to be loved or to have been abused?

We understand that every person we interact with, whether an employee, a cashier, your child's teacher, or the people living under your roof, has these exact needs. We can never assume all of their needs are being met; therefore, judging a person based on the actions we see on the outside, even if directed at us, does not accurately reflect who that person is. We do not know what is going on inside. We, too, have snapped at someone, been short, insulting, or rude. You don't have to go out of your way, but you can avoid reacting and compounding the problem; maybe you can even help.

6. Gratitude - Give Recognition

This is one of my favorites, which I must continually work on. I love it because it feels good to the person giving the recognition and feels even better to the person receiving it. I listened to a podcast with Aubrey Marcus and Super Bowl Champion, and NFL MVP Aaron Rodgers. They said something that had a profound impact on me: "Everyone wants to be seen." On the most basic level, just seeing the person for who they know they are or are trying to become. Acknowledging a person for doing their job is often a great start. Grabbing last-minute items from the grocery store? "Thank you; I

RUDY S. MONTIJO, JR.

appreciate you being here to help me out (especially on holidays or late at night)."

"Your kid's teacher is doing a good job. I appreciate the effort you put into our child's education. It means a lot." (Maybe offer to donate school supplies.)

This will go even further in your relationships. Have a friend who always picks up when you need them? "I don't need anything; I just wanted to let you know how much I appreciate you always talking to me or even listening to me vent. It means a lot." Tell your kids how important they are, tell your partner "thank you," and acknowledge all the small things they do. You will make someone feel amazing, which will make you feel fantastic. If you're having a bad day or are in a funk, nothing will turn it around quicker than doing this. You will feel better, have more energy, and make someone's day.

7. Communicate in a Way That Will Be Received

The way you communicate with someone is everything. Whether it's via text, email, phone, or in person, the medium does not matter. If you want your message to be received, you must communicate in a way that ensures the person will receive it. This is especially important if you're in a leadership position, a coach, a parent, or in a relationship.

Most people talk not to the other person but for themselves. They want to hear their voice or validate their own beliefs, so they talk *to* people, not *with* people. The first rule of communication is to listen, not to speak. Here is a chance to practice your empathy. Listen, ask open-ended questions, then talk in a calm, controlled tone so you're doing your best not to activate their ego or defense wall.

There are anywhere from 50 to 90 players on a football team, each unique and receiving communication differently. While the players need to adapt to the coaching style and methods, the coach must understand how to communicate effectively with certain players if they want to be effective. Some respond to, or even are motivated by, harsh criticism and loud yelling. For others, this immediately raises their defense wall, and they mentally check out. The same is true within an organization.

Conversely, I would tell the players or employees the same thing. Consider how your coach or boss receives feedback best. Are you personalizing something? Despite how it is being spoken, is what is being said true? Is your wall down, so you're receiving the information? If both parties are on the same page with this and using this tool, you have effective communication and progress.

The same principles apply to your partner and kids. Don't know how they would like to receive communication? Simply ask them. They will tell you.

From a *child's* perspective: "When you tell me I don't know something, it makes me feel like an idiot. It would be better if you asked or explained it to me without yelling. Then, I wouldn't get so upset and lash out."

From a *partner's* perspective: "When you raise your voice, it reminds me of a past relationship. It immediately triggers a not-so-pleasant experience. You aren't the same person, but it sends me into my shell. Then, I have to work on coming out and being vulnerable all over again."

Learn about your audience. Understand how they like to be communicated with and do that. You'll get much further and faster and build stronger relationships built on mutual respect and understanding.

8. Patience

We are not all like YOU. We are not built the same. We do not all have the same capacity for multiple projects and stresses. We all have a unique threshold for risk, love, and acceptance. We need to remember this when working with others. Learning how to be patient will also relieve stress.

What is a lack of patience? Lack of patience is a YOU thing. It's a control issue. Someone is not doing something or moving in the direction as fast or in the way you think they should be. That's it. Does thinking of it like that make you sound like an asshole? Sometimes urgency matters, like at work with deadlines, etc., but I'm talking overall. You are building patience. Patience is finite. Which means you only have so much before you lose it. There are two parts to this.

- Understand that patience is like a muscle. You can build and strengthen it. One way to do this is by ensuring you get proper sleep and maintain a proper diet so you're not constantly hungry. Making sure your "other" to-dos and priorities are checked off means you're not wishing you were somewhere else or constantly thinking about what you must do. Having the self-awareness to realize when your patience is being tested and not giving in helps you get through it. (More on this in Chapter 5).

- Patience is finite, so when you know it's gone for the day, accept that it's gone. Don't take on more or agree to something you don't have the patience for. Say no. Recharge or take the time to get your head back to where it needs to be. Sometimes we have to suck it up and be an adult, but often it's our decision. Learn your capabilities and stick to them; remember, we are all different. You're not competing with others; you're trying to be the best version of yourself. I saw a story on social media where a couple came home, and the wife said she only had about five percent left in her. She was at her limit. The husband heard this and said, "No problem, I'll pick up the rest." She communicated, he listened, and he could see and meet her where she was to support her. Tomorrow is another day.

9. Priorities

I definitely took this from Bob Iger. This is also cool because it changes. But what should not change is the number of our priorities. I suggest 3 to 5, understanding that 1 and 2 might be constant. I wrote this on a plane heading back to Phoenix from Grand Junction. My priorities were as follows:

1. My sobriety (this never changes).
2. My kids (although not until Friday because they are with their mom).
3. My main job (which is why I was in Colorado).
4. My passion (Writing this book, advocating for mental health).
5. Health (I will work out, use the sauna, cold plunge, or do something else for my health later today).

I just signed up for an Ironman, so training will also be in the top five within a few months, which means it's non-negotiable. Understanding your priorities will help you focus on what's important to you. You can easily break it down into personal, professional, and physical. You don't need to create a big goal for each. Just start the required daily habit. The goal will materialize automatically if the daily practices are met. If those are not met, what's the point of your goal?

Get laser-focused on your debt, finances, and mental, emotional, and physical health. Prioritize what's essential and what will move the needle, and do that. That's it. Don't deviate. Be consistent.

10. Be Non-Reactive

We are going to react; there's no question about it. We are only human, and we all have our limits. Occasionally, those limits will be tested. However, this doesn't mean we have to fall into the same trap. We can change and create new habits. You can refer to the free STOP pdf to learn how to begin the process of emotional regulation.

(BONUS: Audiobook transcript)

INTERVIEWER: Leadership traits are very interesting, but this is something that you borrowed from someone else, right?

RUDY: Correct. I read a lot, so part of my methodology involves taking key parts from what I read that I found useful or profound and passing that on to my audience. If you follow me on social media or YouTube or sign up for my course, you'll get a lot of great information from books I've read without having to take the time to read the whole book yourself. In this case, I took principles and leadership traits from Ray Dalio and Bob Iger's book, *The Ride of a Lifetime.* The premise behind this is that most people live too much in the gray as far as who they want to be as a person. So, when situations arise, their actions aren't always in alignment with the idea of that person.

I'll give you two examples. I don't make personal plans when I have my kids. It's that simple. There are occasions when I have to for work or trade days, but if you ask me to go on a trip on a weekend when I have my kids, the answer is no. This makes it very easy to stay consistent with them and be the best dad I can be. Like I said, there are exceptions, but 99% of the time, I try to follow this. Every Ironman I've done was on a weekend when I did not have the kids, except for one in Tempe. Even then, they checked on me the day before, got to experience it, but stayed with their mom on race day.

I hear people tell me they want to drink less and get in shape, yet every opportunity or excuse to go out or eat, they take it. They could just as easily create a workout plan, limit themselves to drinking one day a month, and intermittently fast. Don't deviate, and you'll see results. But, as the saying goes, "Don't be upset by the results you didn't get from the work you didn't do." Decide the type of person you want to be. Develop traits that are aligned with that person. Follow it. If you don't, you'll end up being a ship at sea without a compass and map. If this happens, you may end up somewhere you don't want to be, with only yourself to blame.

At Home Exercise: Create your 10 leadership traits that you want to define you as a person. You can borrow some of mine or create your own. Give it some thought.

NOTES:

_____

_____

_____

_____

_____

_____

_____

_____

_____

_____

_____

_____

CHAPTER 4

Integration

in·te·gra·tion /ˌin(t)əˈgrāSH(ə)n/ *Noun: the act or process of combining two or more things so that they work together.*

Creating your own set of leadership traits will act as a compass. They will ensure you are moving in the right direction, even when it does not feel like it. Understanding when and where to apply your traits might seem foreign at first. Most people don't have a set of values they adhere to, so when faced with adversity or a tough decision, they often freeze or make the wrong decision.

In Chapter 3, we discussed that most decisions are not wrong; they are simply learning experiences. Below, we will discuss specific situations in three areas of life. *Professional* refers to your job or career or where you're striving for more. *Physical* includes your health, your current state, and where you want to be. *Personal* covers your relationship with yourself, others, and other personal matters.

Balance is an Illusion

The idea you will one day have a balanced life is false. It is better to get that out of your mind now. The fact is that we all go through seasons in life. We all have a finite amount of time and energy. During different seasons, our energy is devoted to other things. For example, if you're in medical school training to be a doctor. Most of your time will be spent in school, studying, or residency. There is little time for much else during the season. When your kids are younger, in high school, college, or out of the house, they are all different seasons. Each season, a lot of time is spent on work, kids, personal relationships, etc., but it is never "balanced."

The idea isn't to balance your life but to understand where your energy is going and set internal and external expectations. Internal expectations are for understanding boundaries and where your time is going. External meaning is with friends, family, or loved ones, so they also understand they are still significant; you have other things requiring more energy. Most people get it and understand. Remember, communicate this, and it will be received.

How you set up your time and integrate your macro and micro goals will depend on your priorities. We should aim to have around 1-3 prioritized goals in one of three areas of life - our personal, professional, and physical lives. This will help you determine where your energy goes, as it is aligned with your goals. I've used myself as an example while writing this book. The **numbers** represent my macro goals; the **letters** are the micro or daily habits used to obtain each goal.

Professional

1. Repeat Presidents Club: an award reserved for the top-performing professionals of an organization.
   a. Utilize time blocking for efficiency, identify clear targets, and plan to convert new business.
   b. Pre-plan business travel in accordance with targets and have meetings set.
   c. Provide clinical education to at least six hospitals in my territory.

2. Work on Passion Projects.
   a. Continue to develop video course and content.
   b. Finish book and submit to publisher.
   c. Create three speeches. 5 minutes, 20 minutes, and 50 minutes.

Physical

1. Ironman Tempe 2023.
   a. Follow daily/weekly training program.

Personal

1. Sobriety.
   a. Morning prayer and gratitude.
   b. Get all my work done so I can be present and patient when with my kids and family.
   c. Invest time (calls, texts, trips) with close friends who are mutually supportive and aligned.
   d. Make sure I'm rested so I'm not irritable or lack patience.

Now, the integration part comes into play when it's time to get to work and in specific situations. Knowing your leadership traits and macro goals will help you make real-time decisions. Let's say I have my kids, and they're not behaving. I know enough to understand that I'm tired, so my patience is a bit short. That awareness is all I need.

When my son or daughter does something that might cause a reaction, I run through the process:

Situation: My daughter throws her food or has a tantrum in a public store or restaurant.

Initial reaction: Frustration, anger, and anxiety (not acted upon).

Ego/accountability: Ego instructs my ego and my wall to lower. There is no threat here. I also observe what she is doing and how my son is reacting. I become accountable for the situation and the part that I can control. With pride set aside, I take accountability for taking my daughter out when she is tired or hungry. She is only 2; I am 42. She cannot control her emotions, but I can.

Needs/desired outcome: My macro goal is to be patient, loving, and present with my children. The desired outcome in this situation is to calm my daughter. Try to identify her needs and speak to her and my son calmly, not aggravating her or the situation further.

If I can achieve this outcome in this situation, It will also work toward my macro goal of being patient and loving.

Leadership: I know the traits I have adopted. Now, what needs to be applied in this situation? I need to be empathetic to their needs. I need to be patient; they are only toddlers. I need to communicate with them in a way they will understand. This means speaking softly, not yelling or instilling fear, but getting down on their level to understand and probably hold and comfort her. I tell my son that Savanna is tired and we should probably go home so she can rest. My son is now learning by watching how to de-escalate and control his emotions, which I feel is the appropriate response. As he gets older, I can explain more to him.

This example from my life illustrates a broader point. The situation with my kids could just as well have been about a disagreement with a partner or another adult. Similarly, it could have involved interacting with a customer service person while ordering something as simple as a burger, fries, or a salmon salad. The point is, whatever the situation I face, I need to understand my macro goal and the micro (current situation) and follow through with my leadership trait.

(BONUS: Audiobook transcript)

INTERVIEWER: The integration part is clearly an important piece of the whole process. Can you help paint a picture of what this looks like in everyday life?

RUDY: Yeah, the whole E.N.L.I.T.E.N. process is designed to be easy to remember, so you can easily recall and apply the steps. Again, this is covered in detail in the video course, but for now, let's break it down to a relatable situation in our personal life.

I'll piggyback off the first example. So, if you have kids, you want to be a great parent, right? Who doesn't? When your kid acts up, it triggers a response. You might yell or react in a harmful way. The first step is Ego and Accountability, which is self-awareness: Are you reacting because of what they did, or because you're tired, hungry, or had a bad day? Are they hungry, tired, or emotional? Is their action appropriate for their age or level of development?

Second, what needs to happen here? What outcome do I want, and in this case, how do I get the outcome while instilling healthy skills they can learn and eventually apply in their own life? What leadership trait do I want to insert here? I need to be patient, AND I need to be consistent. Now, we are starting to create the *Mental Legacy*.

I'm not going to give parenting advice because that's not my place. However, I will tell you that I try to mix compassion with accountability in my parenting style. The caveat to this is that kids are smart—you start holding them accountable, they will start holding you accountable, which is a good thing.

Another example that can be used for work or a relationship is staying solution-oriented. Things all happen at work or at home that are less than ideal, or we disagree with. What typically happens in these scenarios is we get triggered (lack of control or expectations not met), and then we get angry and complain about the situation. This is when it becomes dangerous, and people say and do things they regret or cause harm to themselves or someone else. (Lack of emotional regulation). If we get past this without being destructive, we can begin to find a solution to the problem. Why not just skip the drama and jump to solving the problem? The boss gives you a task or assignment. Ok, I'll get it done. Disagreement at home? Clarify what was said, make sure each person is heard, and then either ask for or propose a solution.

When you start doing this, you'll accomplish more and save valuable time and energy.

So, in a nutshell, integration is learning how to show up appropriately and in the best possible way in each situation.

Now, I'll finish by saying no one is perfect. I snap, not often, but I do. I have my moments, just like we all do. We are human. When it happens, I will apologize to my kids or whoever and do my part to make it right. I think that's all we can hope for and expect from anyone, regardless of age.

At Home Exercise: Use three real-life scenarios of how you could have or will integrate these tools into your three areas of life: personal, professional, and physical. Be specific and clear. Have your macro and micro outcomes in mind.

NOTES:

_____

_____

_____

_____

_____

_____

_____

_____

_____

_____

_____

CHAPTER 5

Train Your Thoughts

train /trān/ *Verb: teach (a person or animal) a particular skill or type of behavior through practice and instruction over a period of time.*

thought /THôt/ *Noun: An idea or opinion produced by thinking or occurring suddenly in the mind.*

If you've ever been driving, you've likely experienced getting cut off in traffic. In that instant, your reaction can go one of two ways. First, you might immediately feel the urge to honk, make a gesture, or express your frustration vocally. This reaction is neither positive nor productive and can escalate the situation or even lead to dangerous driving. The second reaction is to calmly adjust your driving, slow down if necessary, and continue safely on your way. This reaction is positive. You maintain control over the situation, keep yourself and others safe, and avoid unnecessary stress. Your response in this moment isn't decided then and there; your mindset and previous experiences determine it.

This reaction is made on a subconscious level. 85% of your reactions are from the subconscious. You don't have time to think,

65

Should I get angry or stay calm? You just react. You've probably reacted in similar ways before. You're on autopilot. The goal here is to retrain the mind to respond with positive, productive behavior rather than a destructive, negative one. When this is achieved, transformation is taking place. Can you imagine if 85% of your reactions were propelling you forward in life? Where would you be? What could you accomplish?

The driving analogy is just one example of how people react. We react to situations and events all day, every day. It starts when the alarm goes off: Do we hit snooze or get up? When our boss or co-worker emails us, do we complain and get frustrated, or do we immediately look to problem-solve and be solution-oriented? Our partner comes home after a bad day. Do we compound the problem by reacting negatively, or do we ask how we can support and listen to them?

Each reaction comes with its own set of consequences. If you want immediate results in positivity and progress, I suggest starting by subduing your ego and retraining your thinking. You'll be surprised how quickly your life can turn around.

How to Retrain Your Mind

Self-awareness: You can't change anything unless you know you're doing it. Reading this book will increase your self-awareness tenfold. You can no longer complain and blame without looking at yourself. If you do, you're the problem, not anyone else. When you realize you are in control of your actions, you can react differently. Be patient with yourself. You've been programmed to respond in a certain way for years; creating new neural pathways and embedding your positive traits into your subconscious will take time. Over time, you'll have replaced your old, damaging, destructive software with new, positive, productive software, ready to operate and move you forward.

Meditation: The mind does not differentiate between a thought and reality. To the mind, it's all the same. Meditating on a particular habit will signal to the mind that you've been in that situation before, making it easier to react positively. If you can subject your body to stress and meditate, you'll be able to maintain composure, increase your emotional regulation, and react appropriately more often.

A Formula One driver often sits and closes his eyes, visualizing every turn on the track, training his mind to respond. When he gets in the car and sees the turn ahead, he can react or even anticipate the turn. If you're trying to stay sober and have an event to attend where there will be alcohol, close your eyes and visualize yourself walking into the event. Where is the bar? A waiter offers you a drink. Say, "No, thank you." Play it in your mind first. What does it feel like? What does it smell like? How does it feel to be around alcohol? Now, in real life, it won't be the first time; it will be easier to say no and stick to your plan. You can do this with any situation in life.

The best way to do this is by meditating in a sauna with extreme heat, taking a cold plunge or shower, or when you're physically and mentally exhausted after a challenging workout or long day. The heat or cold-water shock triggers an evoked emotional state. By meditating, keeping calm, and controlling our breathing and thoughts, we are training our minds to react in a controlled fashion, even in moments of stress, which is when we need it most.

This is how special forces and elite athletes train and why they can perform under severe stress repeatedly. That Navy Seal has been shot at in the cold dark of night and stayed up for 24 hours so many times that when they are called to a mission, their mind and body are on autopilot. They react with the most positive, productive, and precise actions designed to keep them safe and accomplish the mission.

That Super Bowl-winning quarterback who drops back and throws a 60-yard pass on target with a 250-pound linebacker charging at him in front of 80,000 people, and their heads ringing from the last hit. They can do this because they have practiced and been in this situation hundreds of times. They have trained their mind and body to react automatically, giving their team an optimal chance to win.

Think about these examples and how you react in your own life, personally, professionally, and physically. Are your reactions and subconscious responses helping you progress or hurting you? Can you imagine the compound effect it would have if your natural reactions in life were positive and productive? You'd be unstoppable and create a forward momentum that's impossible to hold back. This is transformation.

The Science of Positive Neuroplasticity: How Changing Your Thoughts Rewires Your Brain

With its intricate web of neurons and synapses, the human brain is a dynamic organ capable of remarkable adaptability. Scientific research in neuroplasticity has uncovered the astonishing capacity of the brain to reorganize itself in response to experience. Simply put, you can rewire your brain by changing your actions and environment. Changing your environment may not be feasible for everyone at first; this is where the beauty of meditation comes into play. Simply closing one's eyes and picturing a new environment can give a person the same emotions of actually being there. The brain connects the image to the heart, just like when you look at an old picture that makes you smile. Do this with your goals, and you're on your way.

Understanding Neuroplasticity

Neuro means brain. Plasticity is the ability to change. Neuroplasticity is your brain's ability to change—that's it. Contrary to earlier beliefs that the brain's structure was fixed after a certain age, more recent studies prove the brain has the ability to change throughout life. You CAN teach an old dog new tricks, after all.

The Role of Neural Pathways

At the core of neuroplasticity is the concept of neural pathways. Think of a pathway as a road. These roads are formed through repeated thoughts, emotions, and behaviors. The corresponding neural pathways (roads) strengthen when we consistently engage in specific thought patterns and are enforced more by actions. The opposite is also true; neglected or unused pathways weaken and may even start to break down. We can reshape these neural pathways by intentionally altering our thoughts and positively rewiring our brains.

Positive Thinking and the Brain

Positive thinking is not merely a psychological concept; it has tangible effects on the brain's structure and function. Studies using advanced neuroimaging techniques, such as functional magnetic resonance imaging (fMRI), have shown that positive thoughts and emotions activate specific regions in the brain associated with reward, motivation, and emotional regulation. Releasing neurotransmitters, such as dopamine and serotonin, reinforces these positive associations. What this all means is the more your positive thoughts are followed by positive or productive actions, the better you will naturally feel. This compound effect this has on a person's life is profound. It is how momentum works and can exponentially propel you forward.

The Impact of Mindfulness and Meditation

Mindfulness practices, including meditation, have gained popularity for their role in promoting positive neuroplastic changes. The brain does not know the difference between reality and a thought or something that has not happened. If you think of a sad moment in your life and begin to cry, this is why. Or if you daydream and feel like you're falling and jump out of your chair, you'll quickly realize to the brain you were falling or experiencing that sad moment again. These are attached to reactions or emotions in the present.

By meditating, closing your eyes, and simply thinking of what accomplishing your goals looks and feels like, you are attaching a positive emotion to a thought. Where your thoughts go, the body will follow. Attaching positive emotions will strengthen your behavior and further help to positively rewire your brain and create a new road (pathway) to success, whatever that looks like for you.

How to Rewire Your Brain

1. **Acceptance:** Definitively accept what you want to change.

2. **Set Clear Goals:** Establish measurable goals broken down into smaller obtainable goals. Create momentum.

3. **Action:** Start taking action immediately. Do something every day. If you need to run three miles and can only get one mile in, do one mile. If you need to study for two hours but can only get it in 30 minutes, do it in 30 minutes. Do something every day. You're building endurance.

4. **Consistent Repetition:** Repeat the behavior consistently. Repetition is crucial for forming habits. Aim for daily practice to reinforce the behavior.

5. **Anchor to Existing Habits:** Associate the new habit with an existing one. For example, if you want to develop a habit of stretching every morning, do it right after brushing your teeth. Finding your keystone habit will make this more obtainable.

6. **Positive Reinforcement:** Reward yourself when you complete the behavior. Positive reinforcement strengthens the neural pathways associated with the habit. DO NOT reward yourself with negative behavior that will cause digression.

7. **Track Your Progress:** Keep a record of your efforts. This could be a journal, a habit-tracking app, or any other method that helps you monitor your consistency.

8. **Visual Cues:** Use visual reminders or cues to prompt the behavior. This could be a sticky note, a digital reminder, or any visual that connects with the habit.

9. **Patience and Persistence:** Habits take time to develop. Be patient and persistent. It's normal to face challenges, but staying committed to the process is critical.

10. **Social Support:** Share your goals with friends or family who can provide encouragement or join you in developing the same habit. Social support can be a powerful motivator. Cut ties or limit access to those who are not aligned. You don't have to be righteous, but do what is best for you.

11. **Mindfulness and Awareness:** Stay mindful of your actions. Being aware of the habit as you perform it reinforces the connection between the behavior and your intention.

12. **Adaptability:** Be open to adjusting your approach. If a particular strategy isn't working, consider modifying it to suit your lifestyle and preferences better.

13. **Celebrate Milestones:** Celebrate small victories along the way. Recognizing and celebrating progress can help maintain motivation.

By consistently applying these strategies, you can transform a conscious decision into a subconscious habit. Remember that the key is to be patient, persistent, and mindful throughout the process.

(BONUS: Audiobook transcript)

INTERVIEWER: Re-wiring your brain and training your thoughts. I love this part because of the science behind it. I know many people learn differently or need hard facts to really buy in. You explained that aspect in this chapter, but tell us a little about what made you a believer and how your audience can better understand how this is possible for them.

RUDY: Yes! So, I really geek out on this. I find it so fascinating because it's a blueprint for transformation. It comes from the inside out, which is necessary to sustain growth. What I mean by that is many people succeed in a structured environment because they are told what to do. Outside that environment, they fail or digress. Are you following me so far?

INTERVIEWER: Kind of. Do you have an example?

RUDY: Yeah, so there were a lot of guys I played football with in college. Almost all of them were physically fit; we all were in shape, muscular, and looked and felt good. We had coaches, trainers, and a schedule that kept us this way. Fast forward 5 or 10 years after we were done playing football, some guys who were once absolutely jacked and these physical specimens of a man were now 50, 100, 150 pounds overweight, and some were still in shape years later. It's the same for women, too. I have a lot of friends who played soccer and softball in college.

Actually, when I think about it, the women seemed to have maintained their level of discipline much further into life. Shout out to all the female athletes out there. But in this example, the coaches were the structured external environment. When it left, so did the discipline. The people who were internally motivated and developed their own structure were the people who stayed in shape. Because they wanted to, not because they had to. Does that make sense?

INTERVIEWER: Ahhh, yes. That makes sense.

RUDY: Good, and I'm no different. I left college and was lost for a long time. I drank, was out of shape, didn't have a vision or clear goals. It wasn't until I became my own internal coach and wanted it for myself that I was able to find long-term success and change, completing an Ironman at 43. 21 years after I stopped playing college football. Using this method, you slowly start to coach yourself in a positive direction. Personally, professionally, and physically. The way the brain works is just like how you drive home. 85% is on autopilot. It's why you can be on the phone or not really paying attention and drive home. You've done it so many times before; it's just what you know. It's the same for your relationship choices and financial and physical goals.

Imagine this drive now included reading a book every month, working out three days a week, and saving or investing money. If you do this little by little now, your new autopilot is positive, productive behavior. That is re-wiring your brain for long-term success.

INTERVIEWER: So when did this happen to you?

RUDY: I really started seeing this when I started doing triathlons, paying off debt, and finishing up my master's degree. I started checking things off one by one. One assignment from class. One 3-mile run. One credit card. I had a plan for each and did it a little at a time. Now, I want to make it clear I didn't do it without help. One of my best friends,

Mike, gave me financial advice. I listened to him and did what he said. Before I could afford to hire Lewis Elliot as my coach, I followed a training plan I found on the Ironman website. The school has its own structure. But I did the work.

Then, some time goes by, and I've done 2 or 3 triathlons, I've graduated and am a therapist, and I've paid off my debt. I just leveled up from where I was before. Then I got a larger, newer SUV for my kids and a bigger home so we had more room, started a business, completed an Ironman, and finished this book. I leveled up again. I'm not unique or special. I started with less than nothing. I started from rehab with no job and debt. Once I accepted the facts and became accountable, it clicked, and everything changed. Now, this is just how my brain works. For every excuse you give me why you can't do something, I'll show you two ways it's possible. It's just how I see life now.

The main thing I want my audience to understand is that this is possible for them, too. It's possible to get past your traumas, to climb out of that hole, and to be who you are capable of becoming. Unlike me, I don't compare myself to others anymore, and neither should you. But you, and you alone, are responsible for your success and failures—make no mistake: both failure and success are choices.

At Home Exercise: By now, you should be creating more self-awareness and catching your reactions. Write down your new positive, productive thoughts, and intentional responses or actions. This will strengthen the connection between thought and action, reinforcing the positive outcome and helping you build momentum. (You're more likely to do something you write down versus just thinking about it.) For example, when I receive a new email, task, or assignment at work, I will create solutions and plan to respond or act accordingly. (Notice I did not say I won't complain - you want to stay in accountability, which keeps you in control.)

NOTES:

_____

_____

_____

_____

_____

_____

_____

_____

_____

_____

CHAPTER 6

Emotions

e·mo·tion /əˈmōSH(ə)n/ Noun: a natural instinctive
state of mind deriving from one's circumstances, mood,
or relationships with others.

Emotions are complex. They are not black and white and are never what they seem. They require more depth of understanding. For this reason, this is the longest and most in-depth chapter. There are a few concepts I want to go over and provide additional resources if they resonate with you. My video course covers these concepts in much more depth with specific examples.

The first concept is that all emotions stem from two primal emotions: **love** and **fear**.

We all think we know what love and fear mean. At its most basic level, loving someone equates to a deep, emotional, and intimate connection with that person. Fear, at its basic level, is simply being scared of someone or something. These emotions, and the concept that love or fear is what's causing you to react in certain ways in the present, are what I want you to understand and feel, recognizing how it has played a role in your life's decisions and relationships.

Let's start with a common one: controlling behavior. When someone is controlling, they want to dictate both small and large aspects of another person's life. This can be anything from what they wear and who they talk to, to what jobs they take and the duties those jobs require, such as travel, dinners, and work events with both male and female colleagues.

The one who is trying to control is doing so for possibly a couple of reasons, reasons which they are either aware of but most likely unaware of the root cause, so they mask it as love. "I love you so much I just want [xyz] for you." You may have heard this before. The controller is coming from a place of fear, certainly not love. They may love you, but their actions are the product of fear-based thinking and emotions.

A controller is likely insecure, has had a chaotic upbringing, been burned, or lost trust in a previous relationship. So, they are scared; they are fearful of losing you, scared they are not enough, and scared that if they "let" you be you, you'd find someone better. They fear all of this, so they try to "control" the outcome to what THEY desire it to be.

Here is a short list of fear-based characteristics:

- Dictate friends.
- Ghosting (fear of rejection or getting too close).
- Won't let you do things alone, always wants to be together (fear of you meeting someone else when they're not around).
- Separation from family or friends (fear they won't approve and convince a person to leave you).

The problem with these characteristics is that they have nothing to do with the person who is supposedly "loved" and everything to do with the controller's unhealed wounds that are now being projected onto their new partner. The controller's behavior can also stem from a skewed perspective of how they view the world. The world should act and behave according to their ideologies and beliefs shaped by their environment. They outwardly try to control or reject anything that threatens their beliefs out of fear that it might be taken away, deconstructed, or proven false.

Controllers typically have a narrow view of the world, which is why they are often disagreeable and argumentative. They become defensive and reject conversations that challenge them. It is extremely naive to think the world will think like you and share the same beliefs as you when you yourself have not challenged why you believe what you do to begin with. A person raised in New York City or Los Angeles will likely have very different political views from someone raised in Amarillo, Texas, or Cheyenne, Wyoming. California and New York are historically liberal states, while Texas and Wyoming are more conservative. Both are very different from countries in the Middle East or Asia. So, one's belief system is ingrained in them from a very young age. When this is challenged, or when an ideology different from their own is presented, it triggers an emotional and somatic response. Somatic just means you can feel it in your body. It's almost like it's a personal attack, but to that person, that is exactly what it feels like.

The goal is not to persuade anyone to think like us. The goal is to be aware and educated enough to understand why we feel the way we do, and rational enough to have a respectful conversation. You can only control one person, and that is yourself. Failure to see this will end up causing you a lot of anger, resentment, and limit your emotional and mental growth because you're focusing on differences, not similarities. We all share both.

Love, often regarded as the most profound and positive emotion, is a force that binds individuals and societies. It brings out the best in people, allowing us to see past our differences for the greater good. It fosters patience, selflessness, empathy, and compassion. It creates cohesiveness and respect, whether it's giving up your time to help a friend, putting your child's personal desires above your own, or loving yourself enough to live a healthier lifestyle. In a relationship, it can help you accept a person for who they are with no expectation to change. It means supporting what makes them happy, letting them be who they are, and loving them for their past, the person they are today, not who they may or may not be tomorrow.

The closest and strongest relationships I've had, both romantic and friendships, are with those I feel safe with. Safe to share my story without judgment. On the contrary, in relationships where I felt I had to hide things or there was no interest in learning about the experiences that shaped me, I felt resentful, fake, and over time, I became a shell of who I was at the core. Over time, I've learned to love myself and others enough to create a safe space for both people while establishing a deep connection and setting healthy boundaries in the process.

Here is what love can look like in all relationships:

- Loving yourself enough to respect your own boundaries and set healthy boundaries of how you wish to be treated.
- Accepting others, their past, and who they are now.

- Giving with no expectation of getting anything in return.
- Supporting people in their goals, even if that takes time away from you.
- Showing up for others consistently, not just when it's convenient.
- Trusting someone (unless you have a reason) to know they love you enough to do the right thing when you're not around.

The intricate relationship between love and fear is especially clear in personal growth and self-discovery. You often have to face and conquer fear to follow your passions, embrace change, or step outside your comfort zone. At the same time, the drive for these pursuits usually comes from a deep love for yourself and a desire for personal fulfillment and realizing your true potential.

I mentioned earlier that Aubrey Marcus interviewed NFL quarterback Aaron Rogers on his podcast, and Rogers said something that stuck with me: "At the end of the day, people just want to be seen." We all want to be seen for who we are. It doesn't mean you have to agree, but if we can love enough to see past our beliefs into what makes someone else who they are, I think it would be a good start.

Attachments

Attachment Theory, developed by psychologist John Bowlby, shows that the relationships we form early in life greatly influence our connections later on. Attachment styles are behavioral patterns that develop based on how responsive and available our caregivers were in our infancy. These styles affect how we relate to others as adults. I first learned about attachment styles from my therapist. She suggested the book *Attached* by Amir Levine, M.D. and Rachel S.F. Heller, M.A.

There are four main attachment styles: *secure, anxious-preoccupied, dismissive-avoidant, and fearful-avoidant*. Understanding these can help us better understand how we form and manage relationships.

1. Secure Attachment: Secure attachment is considered the healthiest and most adaptive style. It develops when caregivers consistently meet a child's emotional and physical needs, providing a secure base for exploration. Adults with secure attachment styles have positive views of themselves and their partners. They are comfortable with emotional intimacy, trust others easily, and effectively manage relationship conflict. Secure individuals are more satisfied with their relationships and can form lasting connections.

In romantic relationships, securely attached individuals feel confident expressing their needs and emotions. They can navigate both independence and closeness without fear of abandonment. They are supportive and responsive partners, fostering a sense of safety and stability for their loved ones.

2. Anxious-Preoccupied Attachment: Anxious-preoccupied attachment develops when caregivers are inconsistent in meeting a child's emotional needs. Individuals with this attachment style often seek high emotional closeness and approval from their partners. They may worry about abandonment and have a heightened sensitivity to relationship dynamics.

In intimate partnerships, individuals who have anxious-preoccupied attachment styles might display needy behavior, have a deep fear of being rejected, and often need constant reassurance. They could have self-esteem issues and tend to see uncertain situations in a pessimistic light. Even though they long for close connections, their apprehension of being left alone can result in a rollercoaster of emotions, posing challenges to keeping stable relationships.

3. Dismissive-Avoidant Attachment: Dismissive-avoidant attachment arises when caregivers are emotionally unavailable or consistently unresponsive to a child's needs. Individuals with this attachment style often downplay the importance of emotional connections and may prioritize independence. They may have difficulty expressing emotions and may seem emotionally distant.

When applying this to romantic relationships, dismissive-avoidant individuals may struggle with intimacy and find it challenging to trust their partners fully. They often value independence and may be uncomfortable with emotional vulnerability. While they may appear self-sufficient, their avoidance of emotional intimacy can hinder the development of deep and meaningful connections.

4. Fearful-Avoidant Attachment: Fearful-avoidant attachment, also known as disorganized attachment, results from caregivers who are inconsistent or abusive. Individuals with this attachment style often have conflicting desires for closeness and fear of intimacy. They may experience anxiety and discomfort in relationships, unsure whether to seek closeness or withdraw.

Individuals with fearful-avoidant attachment styles often show unpredictable behavior when forming close bonds with others. They may have trouble trusting people and fear getting hurt. While they yearn for connection, they often struggle with managing their emotions, which can lead to difficulties in establishing and maintaining stable relationships.

Relationship Patterns

Attachment styles play a crucial role in shaping relationship patterns throughout life. Understanding one's attachment style and that of one's partner can provide insights into communication dynamics, emotional needs, and potential challenges. Here's how each attachment style may manifest in relationship patterns:

- **Secure Attachment in Relationships:**
    - Healthy and stable relationships with good communication.
    - Comfortable with both independence and intimacy.
    - Effective conflict resolution skills.
    - Trust in oneself and one's partner.

- **Anxious-Preoccupied Attachment in Relationships:**
    - Constant need for reassurance and validation.
    - Fear of abandonment, leading to clingy behavior.
    - Difficulty managing uncertainty in relationships.
    - Tendency to interpret ambiguous situations negatively.

- **Dismissive-Avoidant Attachment in Relationships:**
    - Valuing independence over emotional intimacy.
    - Difficulty expressing emotions and avoiding vulnerability.

- ○ Tendency to prioritize self-sufficiency.
- ○ Struggling with trust and emotional connection.

- **Fearful-Avoidant Attachment in Relationships:**
  - ○ Conflicting desires for closeness and fear of intimacy.
  - ○ Unpredictable behavior in relationships.
  - ○ Difficulty trusting others and fear of being hurt.
  - ○ Challenges in emotional regulation.

Changing Attachment Styles

While attachment styles are often established in early childhood, they are not fixed. Individuals can develop more secure attachment patterns through self-awareness, personal growth, and positive relationship experiences. Here are some strategies for shifting toward a more secure attachment style:

- **Secure Attachment:**
  - ○ Foster self-awareness and emotional intelligence.
  - ○ Engage in open and honest communication in relationships.
  - ○ Seek therapy to address any unresolved issues or traumas.

- **Anxious-Preoccupied Attachment:**
  - ○ Develop self-esteem and self-reliance.
  - ○ Challenge negative thought patterns and insecurities.
  - ○ Practice mindfulness and stress-reduction techniques.

- **Dismissive-Avoidant Attachment:**
  - ○ Explore and express emotions in a safe and supportive environment.

o Gradually build emotional intimacy in relationships.

o Learn to trust and healthily rely on others.

- **Fearful-Avoidant Attachment:**
  o Seek therapy to address past traumas and unresolved issues.
  o Develop coping mechanisms for managing anxiety in relationships.
  o Gradually build trust and intimacy with supportive partners.

You can change your attachment style. Because these are deeply rooted in childhood, I would suggest a combination of ketamine therapy and psychotherapy with a therapist trained in Internal Family Systems and EMDR. This shift has moved me from anxious attachment to a place where I've seen a profound effect on what I look for in a partner and in myself.

I highly recommend taking my video course to better understand what this looks like in your life and how to move toward a secure attachment if you're willing.

(BONUS: Audiobook transcript)

INTERVIEWER: Emotions. This is a tough subject because, as a reader, I just feel like there is so much that is out of my control. I mean, everyone has emotions. How do you get to the point where you can understand which emotions are good and bad... it just seems incredibly complicated, right?

RUDY: Emotions are a tough one, for sure. It's like comparing an alcoholic to someone who is addicted to food. For an alcoholic, you just remove the alcohol right, don't drink, and then work on underlying issues, but every person has to eat food. You have to eat every day to live. You can't just stop eating, but you can completely cut out alcohol. So you have to navigate which foods are healthy and which are hurting, so from that perspective, yes, it's incredibly complex.

Simon Sinek talks about discovering your "why." That's what we focus on with emotions. Again, the video course goes much deeper into this, but I'll try and simplify it quickly. It's important to understand why you feel the way you do. It comes from something from somewhere, most likely childhood, a past relationship or experience. So, when something upsets you, ask yourself, *Why am I upset?* If something makes you feel threatened or insecure, ask yourself, *Where is this coming from?* I'll give a very clear example for everyone.

Your cell phone. You're having lunch or dinner with someone, and someone sets their phone upside down so you can't see the screen. Each person will have a different feeling from that depending on their past. One person might think, *What are they hiding,* or *What do they not want me to see?* A person who feels like this is likely insecure and was cheated on or has trust issues. Another person thinks, *Oh, they don't want to be distracted and want to give me their attention so they can focus.* It's the same action but two different emotions or reactions.

My goal isn't to help you not feel emotions; it's to understand where they are coming from so you can make a logical decision based on facts, not emotion. Separating emotion from logic is a skill that can be learned.

Finally, don't think in terms of good and bad emotions. They're just emotions. Try not to attach a positive or negative meaning to them. Always give yourself some grace and just understand that you're human. We all have emotions and insecurities. I just want people to have the ability to understand themselves better so they can make choices that help and not hurt them.

At Home Exercise: Try to figure out your attachment style, what triggers you, and what creates fear and defensiveness. Try to identify the root cause and work on changing it by following the steps of E.N.L.I.T.E.N., working in the *Mental Legacy* video course or seeing a therapist who is IFS (Internal Family Systems) informed and EMDR certified.

NOTES:

CHAPTER 7

Nurture

nur·ture /ˈnərCHər/ *Noun: The process of caring for and encouraging the growth or development of someone or something.*

Life isn't easy, and it's not supposed to be. We all face adversity. Whatever you're going through, or have gone through, doesn't make you special or unique. You won't get a job or pay rent because of what you've gone through. That's entitlement, and it's not how life works. However, that doesn't mean we don't need help along the way. It doesn't mean we look down on others when they are in a low spot. The best part of overcoming adversity is being able to help someone else get through the same thing. That's how my journey began, in a room at Alcoholics Anonymous. One person who found sobriety helps another who is looking for it. We can use our experiences to relate and help others.

This is nurturing. This creates a level of compassion and empathy that I feel the world desperately needs. But you can't help anyone if you can't help yourself. You are the most critical person in your life, not your kids, spouse, or parents. Therefore, these steps are crucial. They give you the skills to manage your life, emotions, career, relationships, finances, and health. Then, you can help others. These skills are used for you first, and then you can pass them on to someone else. Nurture yourself so you can grow, then pass along healthy habits to someone else.

People often say things like, "I'd do anything for my kids or my spouse." But would they really? Consider an overweight parent in poor health who can't run around and play with their children. They're not only missing out on life but also at risk of heart attack, diabetes, and other illnesses that could lead to severe disability or even death. Think about those heated arguments with your partner where you lose your temper and say things you can never take back. What are you doing to regulate your emotions and communicate healthily? Do your kids witness this? Are you teaching them that it's okay? You might complain about the cost of vacations, gym memberships, or eating healthy, but is there always beer in the fridge or money for a Starbucks run? Do you want to get ahead, or do you just complain? Are you willing to sacrifice a little to return to school, learn a new trade or skill to make extra money, or start a side business? Take a good look in the mirror. Be accountable. Lower your ego and start from the beginning in every situation. This is about nurturing yourself, and it's an ongoing process.

Nurturing simply means continuing to work on yourself while being patient with others. Thats all. Nurture your mind, your body, and your spirit. Do this, and everything else will fall into place.

Conclusion

Congratulations! You made it! I hope you have gained some valuable insight and actionable steps by sharing my story and experiences. By following the E.N.L.I.T.E.N. system, you can hopefully begin your own transformative journey through personal growth and self-awareness.

Here's a quick summary:

- **Ego:** You've learned the importance of recognizing and managing your ego. This understanding is crucial in making objective decisions, enhancing relationships, and maintaining a balanced perspective in life's challenges.

- **Needs:** Identifying and addressing your goals on a macro and micro level. Putting a plan in place to get your desired outcome in specific situations, which in turn will help you accomplish your goal.

- **Leadership:** By developing your own set of leadership traits, you've discovered how to be a more effective leader, not just in professional settings but in all areas of life, including personal relationships.

- **Integration:** The integration of these principles into everyday life is vital. You've explored how to apply your leadership traits and understanding of ego and needs in real-life situations, leading to more thoughtful and effective responses.

- **Training Your Thoughts:** Retraining your mind to respond positively in various situations is a powerful tool. You've learned techniques for breaking negative thought patterns and replacing them with constructive ones.

- **Emotions:** This section helped you understand the complex nature of emotions and their profound impact on decision-making. You've learned the significance of emotional regulation and how it can improve both personal and professional relationships.

- **Nurture:** Finally, nurturing yourself and others is a continuous process. You've discovered how self-care and personal development are not selfish acts but essential for growth. Nurturing leads to a more compassionate, empathetic, and fulfilling life.

You can use these steps repeatedly until they become second nature. You'll find yourself correcting your language, changing your habits, and transforming into the person you're capable of being. And it won't stop there. Once you start, you'll open new doors in your mind and heart; your growth will increase exponentially. You'll set new goals, raise the bar, and climb higher each time. You'll be enlightened and ready to leave your *Mental Legacy*.

THANK YOU FOR READING MY BOOK!

Thank you for reading my book! Here are a few free bonus gifts.

Scan the QR Code Here:

I appreciate your interest in my book and value your feedback as it helps me improve future versions of this book. I would appreciate it if you could leave your invaluable review on Amazon.com with your feedback. Thank you!

Made in the USA
Las Vegas, NV
04 April 2024

88242853R00066